Published by
The Architecture Foundation

Ground Floor East / 136-148 Tooley Street
London SE1 2TU
www.architecturefoundation.org.uk

Edited by
Sarah Ichioka and Moira Lascelles

Designed by
Work + Play

South Kilburn Studios / 2a Canterbury Road
London NW6 5SW
www.weareworkandplay.com

First published May 2012

Price: £5

CONTENTS

FOREWORD

Mark Brearley, Design for London

This publication celebrates a big project, in a small building–a big project that does two good things at once. Firstly, it is a gift to its locality. South Kilburn Studios has been a catalyst for changed perceptions; the prompter of an exciting buzz, and renewed interest from locals, visitors and authorities who should care but sometimes don't. It has become a signpost to Kilburn – alerting everyone to the big potential of the place. These are all attributes of a great meanwhile project.

The idea of the project was put forward by a start-up business–Practice Architecture – and we are already seeing the successes of their programme that helps other small creative businesses flourish, and encourages them to share their expertise and their energy with local people. The project is all about the people it has pulled together, and the blast of enthusiasm they have brought to a place that welcomes it, that wants fresh things to happen, that wants sparks to turn into flames that light up new opportunities.

The second good thing the South Kilburn Studios project does is show us how we can exploit London's wealth of creativity. This is where the project gets big. The whole endeavour has been driven along by creative people drawn from our city's vast reservoir of talent and enthusiasm.

It helps us realise that London is the local community. London's creative resource, in all its breathtaking diversity and world-beating excellence, can be drawn in by all people in all places. What's going on in South Kilburn helps us get the message that the design and creative capability in our community wants to help good things happen across the city. If we can get that realisation to spread, then more wonderful things will happen in other localities across London.

Already in our city we are seeing a growing community of architects, designers, and other creative professionals putting their skills to work in focused, low-cost and high impact ways. Their projects range from community planting to events focused on reactivating markets and high streets, shop front upgrades and the sparky reuse of vacant properties to create space for community and business. They demonstrate that every vacant building or unused piece of land can be turned into something attractive and useful.

For architects and designers this expands their role from building shapers and aesthetes with ideals, to practitioners of public life, helping with the challenges facing everyday places, and people all over London who want good things to happen in their locality.

South Kilburn Studios is a taster–an exemplary project that heralds an exciting approach to local place-based regeneration that is taking hold in London–and all who have worked to make it happen should be proud.

INTRODUCTION

Sarah Ichioka, The Architecture Foundation

"Old ideas can sometimes use new buildings. New ideas must use old buildings."
- Jane Jacobs [1]

What the venerable urbanist Jacobs meant by her oft quoted statement is that the ability of a place to adapt to changing conditions, to evolve as a viable, diverse socio-economic ecosystem, can depend as much upon inexpensive, run-of-the mill building stock as upon shiny new infrastructure or stunning period architecture. Jacobs's ecosystem was 1950s New York City. In our current context of austerity-squeezed and heritage-worshipping contemporary Britain, cheap and ugly buildings arguably have the competitive advantages of being readily available and relatively free from the well-intentioned stifling of preservation campaigns.

In the cheap and ugly category of contemporary buildings, it is hard to think of a less-glamorous, or more ubiquitous, typology than the 'portable cabin'[2]. Less cool than the shipping container, less iconic than the prefab housing estate, the portable cabin is perhaps the architectural equivalent of the hi-visibility vest: an element so present in the urban landscape that it has become invisible. An example of this humble typology –a vacant unit that had previously housed the office of the South Kilburn New Deal for Communities (a vestige of Blair-era urban regeneration), for which subsequent plans to develop a new health centre had stalled (a victim of lean times) – was the starting point for the project addressed in this book.

Practice Architecture – a sprightly design-build firm, directed by Lettice Drake and Paloma Gormley, in close association with Henry Stringer and Olga Winterbottom – had previously proven themselves talented activators of banal building types. When we approached them to pitch ideas for part of the South Kilburn public art programme, alongside three other architects, Practice's most acclaimed project to date was the social activation of a multi-storey car park in Peckham, South London.

As a non-profit agency promoting innovation and social engagement in the built environment, The Architecture Foundation (AF) aims to pilot new initiatives through which architecture and design can enrich lives. The brief from the AF, and our project partners, the South Kilburn Neighbourhood Trust and Brent Council, was simple, but complex. The invited architects were asked to transform the empty Council-owned structure into a site of social and cultural exchange, which would attract new people to the area while also creating uses and activities of genuine value to those who already lived there. The transformation had to happen quickly – due to funding restrictions – involve young local residents, and be executed at minimal cost. Practice won the tender, and went to work immediately.

[1] Jane Jacobs, The Death and Life of Great American Cities, 1961, London: Pimlico (edition from 2000), p. 201.

[2] Or 'portacabin', a name fiercely defended against generic use by Portakabin Ltd

Volunteers at work painting
the facade of the old portable
cabin

Late-capitalist culture has a particular obsession with the makeover, seeking stories that
can neatly be summed up in two images: the 'before' and 'after'. The culture of architecture is by no means immune to this tendency. We should resist this snapshot approach
to architectural assessment, and insist that more reviews of buildings take place well after
they have folded into the rhythms of everyday use; aiming 'to represent the realities [the
architect is] complicit in creating post-occupancy, as facts, not feats'[3]. In this respect, it
is fortunate that this book is published more than a year after the South Kilburn Studios
first opened to the public, as the intervening period allows reflection upon their day-to-
day operations as opposed to the aesthetics of the pre and post.

Indeed, in assessing the South Kilburn Studios project, the change in how the building *looks* is perhaps one of the least significant aspects. Although Practice Architecture
does have an aesthetic sensibility – immediately evident in, for example, the new light
box atop the building that announces activities inside – their strongest contributions
were programmatic and operational, rather than formal. Working closely with AF curator
Moira Lascelles, Practice choreographed four weeks of hands-on internal demolition
and construction with the help of seventy volunteers. Most importantly, the architects
proposed the business model. The former offices have now become thirteen studios
that host a diverse range of creative start-up businesses (one third from Brent), each
of which – in lieu of rent – mentor a local young person, a 'trainee', helping them
build a portfolio of transferable skills. Further increasing the possibilities for substantive
exchange within the Studios, the public – local and citywide – are invited in for monthly
workshops and open house events.

After a successful six-month start, the Studios' lease on the building was extended by
a further six months, and then again by one year; we at the AF hope it will last even
longer. The essential thing is not that this cheap old building has become more beautiful,
or that it is worth more in real estate terms. Rather, that through programmatic transformation, and with minimal subsidy, the Studios are generating new activity and social
value, becoming an active element contributing to and being integrated in the South
Kilburn ecosystem.

3 Rem Koolhaas, Post-Occupancy, Domus d'Autore, 24 May 2006

SOUTH KILBURN
TODAY AND TOMORROW

Alex Hearn, Brent Council

Watching a film made by one of the South Kilburn Studio tenants, I was struck by a comment made by a teenager living on the estate. Asked what he disliked most about South Kilburn, he replied that it was too small, that it should be bigger. It was as if the juxtaposition of the big blocks on one side of the road and the Victorian terraces on the other created a mental barrier – these were his city limits.

I believe that our challenge in South Kilburn is for it to blend in – for it to become the next ten or twenty streets of this corner of London. Robust and understandable streets ought to allow people to walk out of their front door and get to places for shopping or for working or for learning or for playing. When we're done, it shouldn't be referred to as an estate. Once upon a time, streets were built. They had straight lines, front doors and the odd row of trees. Then, suddenly, building in straight lines became difficult.

When one looks at South Kilburn from above, it has an obvious triangular shape. One sees a strange mess of big blocky buildings at 45° angles to engineered roads. Around it, one sees distinct lines of roofs, distinct lines of green and distinct lines of streets. The 1950s planners, engineers and 'architects' certainly made their mark on this part of the city. Between the streets, mansion blocks and tree-lined avenues of Maida Vale, War-wick Avenue and Queen's Park, the incision of 18-storey Bison blocks, raised walkways and dead ends was made. Middle class architects and planners living in Victorian and Georgian terraces once again experimented on the poor. They knew what was good for them.

Sixty years on, the area is disproportionately over-represented on measures of deprivation. 90 per cent of residents rent their homes from the council; the area is within the top 10 per cent of the 2011 Index of Multiple Deprivation. Statistically, South Kilburn residents are poorer, with fewer qualifications and lower life expectancy than their counterparts across London. Some live in the worst quality housing and often experience over-crowding.

I firmly believe that these socio-economic conditions are exacerbated by the abysmal urban structure and experimental housing design. The development or regeneration process has lost sight of the intrinsic quality of ordinariness for housing.

Brent Council has now embarked on a phased programme of providing good new homes for those living in South Kilburn. This isn't a typical estate regeneration project. We don't move people out, knock down and re-build and then move them back. Instead, because the programme is phased, we offer tenants new homes, and they only have to move once. We aren't replacing an old estate with a new estate, designed by a single

1

1: South Kilburn is located in North West London.

2: South Kilburn Studios sits in the context of the Peel Precinct and is adjacent to the somewhat more affluent area of Queens Park.

2

'regeneration' architect. We take a lot of the development risk. We employ the architects, we apply for planning permission and therefore we retain the control over the quality of the new development.

Alongside our partners at the South Kilburn Neighbourhood Trust, the plan is to provide new homes for 1250 existing households in South Kilburn. In addition to this, we'll provide another 1250 homes for market sale or shared ownership. Blessed with the inherent high values of the area, the former is paid by the latter, and this helps us to correct the predominance of rented council accommodation.

It is absolutely in our interest to attract owner occupiers into the area, so the homes that we sell need to be better than anything else on the market, the local schools need to be good, there needs to be enough doctors and dentists, we need some good shops and we need to provide and maintain good parks. All of these features need to be in the right place.

Of course this will all take time, and we probably won't be completed for ten or fifteen years. It's a process, not an event and it's important we don't lose sight of that.

Surrounded by hundreds of millions of pounds of real-estate, South Kilburn Studios is part of that process and arguably the most exciting project that has happened yet. It's on a human and real scale, it's slightly scruffy and anarchic and it's full of talented people, doing proactive things and helping to inspire some of the young people of the area. Long may it continue. Well, as long as the roof stays intact.

THE SOUTH KILBURN PUBLIC ART PROGRAMME

Sarah Butler, South Kilburn Neighbourhood Trust

South Kilburn Neighbourhood Trust and the London Borough of Brent established the South Kilburn public art programme because they recognised the potential for art and creativity to play a vital role in the regeneration of South Kilburn. In August 2010, I was appointed as South Kilburn Creative Coordinator, charged with delivering a public art programme that would engage communities, build partnerships, develop skills and enhance the local environment. The programme, which consisted of five commissions, ran from August 2010 to April 2011, and was funded by South Kilburn Neighbourhood Trust through the New Deal for Communities.

South Kilburn is undergoing significant long-term physical change. It is also an area with high levels of social deprivation and a range of associated challenges. There is an impressive amount of activity locally: youth groups, arts activities, training programmes, employment and health support, and a lot of passionate and dedicated local people making real differences to the area and to people's lives. My challenge was to create a sustainable programme that added another dimension to the activity within, and the regeneration of, South Kilburn.

I have seen again and again how the arts can inspire and connect people and communities, and how artists can create innovative, and beautiful, interventions within spaces. My background is in literature and participatory arts practice, and I bring a passion for the everyday stories and experiences of places to my commissioning. I believe that regeneration needs to build the skills, confidence and aspirations of local people as well as improve the physical environment, and that arts programmes are well placed to contribute to this agenda. That said I am wary of instrumentalising art, and demanding that it deliver social outcomes over and above artistic ones. The most inspiring, and impactful, 'art in regeneration' work I have seen is the result of brave commissioning and open briefs; projects that do not demand tick-box outcomes, but instead give artists opportunities to work in depth, over significant periods of time, and with the freedom and support to take risks, in order to create work that is genuinely in and of and from that place.

For South Kilburn public art programme, I commissioned five projects, each of which aimed to work with, and listen to, people who lived and worked in the area. Each commission was as open and flexible as possible within the programme constraints.

WORKSHOP 24...

was an 'empty shop' project, delivered by the Empty Shop Network, which took over an unused unit in the Peel Precinct (adjacent to South Kilburn Studios), and created a new, neutral space for people to come together to explore and be inspired by South Kilburn and each other.

workshop24.tumblr.com

BRENT ARTS THERAPIES SERVICE...

in partnership with Emergence, led an Arts in Health project as part of the programme. They commissioned two artists, Julie Bagwash and Tamar Whyte – who identify with personality disorder – to create a new artwork in collaboration with South Kilburn residents experiencing mental health difficulties.

southkilburnproject.moonfruit.com

SOUTH KILBURN SPEAKS...

was a poetry and public art commission, coordinated by The Poetry School. Three poets, Aoife Mannix, Niall O'Sullivan and Simon Mole, worked with over 100 local people to create new work.

Artist Andy Edwards designed and produced for building site hoardings and permanent installation.

southkilburnspeaks.wordpress.com

EVOLVE 01...

was a commission for local film-maker and free-runner Karen Palmer.
Local young people took part in a series of Parkour (free-running) and film-making workshops, and Karen created *Evolution*, a cutting-edge interactive film inspired by Parkour, which premiered at the Tricycle Theatre in February 2011.

evolve01.com

SOUTH KILBURN STUDIOS...

South Kilburn Studios was the result of a commission to reanimate the site of the former New Deal for Communities offices, known as 'the portacabins', and to find a way for the public art programme to respond to the significant levels of unemployment locally. The offices were earmarked for development, but were destined to remain empty for at least a year, triggering concerns about vandalism and the negative impact on the local area of a disused space. I approached The Architecture Foundation, and together we commissioned Practice Architecture to create South Kilburn Studios: thirteen creative studios, offered for a limited time period at no rent, with associated traineeships for young people, and a central space to be used for a programme of free workshops for local residents.

I am still in awe of what The Architecture Foundation and Practice Architecture managed to achieve on a limited budget and within an extraordinarily tight timescale. Their commitment and determination, coupled with that of Alex Hearn from Brent Council, gave this project strong foundations, which have been built on by the passion and energy of the tenants and their trainees. We wanted South Kilburn Studios not only to animate and enhance the physical environment, but also to provide opportunities for small, start-up businesses, and for local young people to develop skills, contacts, and confidence to work within the creative industries.

It has been a pleasure to watch the project flourish, and see it have a real impact for those involved. South Kilburn Studios has a wider legacy too: it has demonstrated to the programme stakeholders the impact that ambitious arts commissioning can have, and the role such projects can play in a wider regeneration programme.

South Kilburn public art programme was an ambitious programme, realised within tight constraints. As with any project, there are lessons to be learnt, and things I would do differently next time, but I am proud to have made these five commissions happen. I would like to extend a huge thank you to all the artists and organizations who worked on the programme, to the hundreds of local people who got involved, and to South Kilburn Neighbourhood Trust and the London Borough of Brent for their commitment to embedding arts and creativity into the ongoing regeneration of South Kilburn.

1: Team meetings became an integral part of Studio life.

2: The studio sign lit at night.

3: Weekly workshops and monthly open studios animate the studios and allow it to touch a wider community beyond the tenants and trainees involved in the project.

1

3

THE IDEA AND THE BUILD

Practice Architecture

THE BRIEF

Think of a new use for, redesign and renovate a delapidated building.

The programme should involve young people and employment and will run for six months.

FIRST THOUGHTS

Simple integrated idea that provides tangible benefits for local people (not just a flash in the pan).

REFINE THE INFRASTRUCTURE:

ENSURE SKS IS REALISTIC AND USEFUL FOR ALL INVOLVED

Talk to studio organisations

Research apprenticeships and accreditation

Talk to local organisiations

MUTUALLY SUPPORTIVE AND SELF-SUSTAINING

Low-income young designers with transferable skills

Local unemployed young people

Dilapidated, empty building

STUDIOS!

DEVELOP FINAL DESIGN

Finding playful low-cost solutions for: lighting, signage. flooring, and exterior

DESIGN CONCEPT

De-institutionalise the space creating a functional clean slate

Create shared facilities that encourage an internal community

Use the facade to communicate what is going on inside

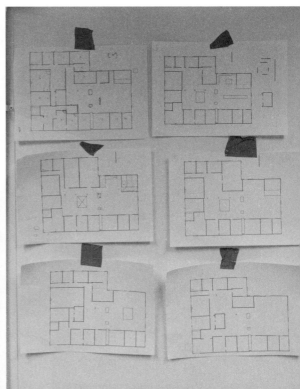

THE SOCIAL INFRASTRUCTURE:

Tenants from different disciplines

Trainees from South Kilburn

Provide hands-on experience and a portfolio of work at the end of thetraineeship

Weekly public workshops

SOUTH KILBURN STUDIO

THE DESIGN

24-metre-long light box containing a cinema style message board

13 naturally-lit studios looking onto a large shared space

Functional timber floor, white walls, gold shutters

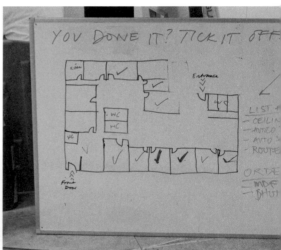

RECRUITMENT

TENANTS

WEBSITES

FLYERING

LOCAL PRESS

PASSERS-BY

TRAINEES

JOB CENTRE

LOCAL PRESS

LOCAL COMMUNITY
ORGANISATIONS

PASSERS-BY

BUILD

SUPPORT

CONTRACTORS

BUILDERS'
MERCHANTS

VOLUNTEER BUILDERS

CONTRACTORS

ARCHITECTURE
STUDENTS

PAINTING AND
DECORATING
STUDENTS

LOCAL PASSERS-BY

COLLABORATORS

WILL SHANNON

OLGA WINTERBOTTOM

ALEX RENNIE

3 WEEKS TO...

REMOVE CARPETS, REMOVE AND MOVE WALLS
MAKE ON-SITE OFFICE/BEDROOM
STRIP EXTERNAL PAINT
PAINT ALL INTERNAL WALLS
PAINT FACADE
LAY PLY FLOOR
CUT LETTERING
BUILD LIGHTBOX UNITS
LIFT LIGHTBOX ONTO ROOF
FIX THE ROOF LEAKS
REWIRE ENTIRE BUILDING
PAINT SHUTTERS GOLD
BRAZE COPPER LETTER RACKS
PAINT AND MOUNT LETTERING
INSTALL KITCHEN
EXTERNAL LANDSCAPING

TENANTS AND TRAINEES

The selection process to find the first tenants and trainees for the Studios was something that we were keen to get right. We knew that the mix of the creatives taking up residence would be key to the success of the project. We also knew that the prospect of free studio space would be very popular and we were keen to find people who would take the 'pay back' of training a local young person in Brent in their profession seriously.

We launched an open call for tenants with just a two-week timeframe to respond to. We received over a hundred applications to be involved with the project from artists, to film-makers to photographers. Applications came from those living just streets away from the studio building and those living across London.

The core team for the project went through a shortlisting process deciding on tenants that we felt would be able to offer the most tangible, transferable and useful skills to ensure future employment. We envisaged that trainees would produce a strong portfo-lio of work during their time at the studios that would show the practical skills they had acquired and been able to refine over the six-month period. It was our belief that in order to ensure this we would need to create a diverse range of traineeships that offered real potential for young people to enter the creative industry of their choice.

After two solid days of interviews we were pleased with the range, diversity and quality of the tenants we selected, all of whom seemed committed and excited by the prospect of taking on a trainee. Studios were assigned based on the size and nature of their business and a week later they moved in!

The task to match them with trainees began. Unlike the call for tenants, our call for trainees proved more challenging. We were looking for young people aged 18-25, living in the borough of Brent, who wished to pursue a career in the creative industries and would commit to a two afternoons a week to a traineeship at South Kilburn Studios.

We held an open day, reached out to Brent's network of employment services, including the job centre, approached local youth centres, used social media platforms and distrib-uted flyers to houses and organisations in the local area.

It would be misleading to say the process was easy; though what we were offering seemed to be attractive – free training with very promising start up businesses - we were at the same time reaching out to a community that were often disengaged, lacked structure and would have to take a leap of faith to become involved.

Despite the challenges, we got there in the end; application forms started to come in by email, my hand and by post. The matching process was relatively easy, trainees had to select the profession they were keen to engage in. After a short, informal interview, the tenant woudl accept them into the programme.

Just three weeks into the Studios being open we had thirteen tenants and thirteen trainees.

Tenants:
Jacob Tomkins
Dan Rolfe Johnson

Trainee:
Francisco Rebello

Working with a
trainee has been
challenging at
times and what
has struck us is
that you become
invested in that
persons future
not just profes-
sionally but
personally too.

Tenant:
Caren Owen

Trainee:
George Allawi

I have watched
George grow
and become a
real part of the
Studios during his
traineeship here.
Putting together
the final show
was a real
achievement
and something
that I feel gave
him a confidence
that will inform
his future
career path.

Tenant:
Jonathan Nyati

Trainee:
Pierre Blaire

The Studios have really brought a new energy to South Kilburn. Having grown up here it is great to finally see a creative hub emerge among the usual provision of shops, housing and youth facilities.

Tenants:
Will Shannon
Kieren Jones

Trainees:
Ree Esen
Josh Wilton-Regan
(not pictured)

We were excited by structuring our traineeship programme to include a variety of different crafts-men and makers to expand our trainee's network and horizons. The best bit was we were learning too!

Tenant:
Pat Victor

Trainee:
Sarah Nansambadah

"

The Studios were quite literally the best thing that happened to me. having a space to run my start-up business from has meant that I have been able to grow and expand – something that wouldn't have been possible in my previous situation.

"

Tenant:
Ben Stefanski

Trainee:
Oliver Zanker

After working with Oliver I was able to introduce him to some contacts in the music industry and he has now started as a producer.

I guess that is exactly what the studios are about!

Tenants:
Tatiana von Preussen
Catherine Pease
Jessica Reynolds

Trainee:
Jack Brindley

We were lucky enough to be so busy that we took on multiple trainees. The Studio environment really worked for us and enabled us to expand our business while passing on skills to the next generation.

Tenants:
Mike Massaro
Kit Oates
Eleanor Kelly

Trainee:
Faith Galiwango

Being able to create a fully functioning photographic studio in the main space meant we could offer Faith hands on experience of assisting on shoots.

Tenant:
Daniel Thomas

Trainee:
Ravi Chandarana

What is special about the Studios is that you are part of a wider creative community. I really enjoy working in this environment with other creatives –ideas are endless. In addition being able to mentor other young minds in the community where I grew up is amazing to be a part of.

Tenant:
Emily Evans

Trainee:
Samiah Ahmed

The events and workshops offered by the Studios gave Samiah the chance to interact with the other trainees and gain other valuable organisational and event management skills.

WORKSHOPS AND OPEN STUDIOS

1

2

1: vPPR staged this installation in the Peel Precinct close to the Studios, which attracted widespread attention.

2: Emerging band Clean Bandit played at a monthly open studio themed around music.

3: Young people showing off the costumes and head gear they had created during a fashion upcycling workshop.

4: Trainee Tee working to 'bodge' a stool during the Urban Bushcraft workshop, run by Kieren Jones and William Shannon.

5: Julio Rebello shows off his interactive DJ and video booth at the final trainee show.

4

5

THE FUTURE

Moira Lascelles, The Architecture Foundation
and Caren Owen, Can Can Productions

Moira Lascelles, Curator, Special Projects, The Architecture Foundation, and Caren Owen, South Kilburn Studios Manager, discuss the successes and challenges of the Studios model and how the project has evolved since the day-to-day running has been handed over from the AF to Caren, from Can Can Productions one of the founding tenants of SKS.

ML: I find it hard to quantify success when talking about South Kilburn Studios. I always saw the project from the very beginning as an experiment and one that was reliant on the people involved to make it work. I feel that each tenant-trainee relationship has had its successes and challenges along the way. Would you agree?

CO: Yes definitely. There are of course stand-out examples like Pierre and Junior who have managed to get into full-time employment through their traineeships at SKS. And then there are those who have had their own smaller achievements, such as presenting an idea to a room full of strangers, writing a CV, or even just turning up on time! All of these smaller achievements are in my eyes successes too.

ML: For sure. I think the relationship between the tenant and the trainee was integral to making the traineeships work and it was interesting seeing all the individual stories unfold. I guess one of the things I would have liked to have provided more of was training for the tenants to deal with mentorship situations that at times could prove to be pretty challenging. We did try but unfortunately our budget only really stretched to one session! I know lots of tenants struggled with trainees not communicating, or at times just not showing up.

CO: Naturally the project is not witout its downfalls but we're committed to doing our best within the bounds of the project. For example, we have expanded the public programme of events and workshops to reach a wider audience. We will soon offer a six-week music production training course as we saw that the one-off workshop format was only offering people a glimpse of the skills they could acquire.

ML: The public programme was certainly something we saw as integral to South Kilburn Studios and one that would make the project more of a resource for the local area. We had been confined to working with young people aged 18-25 in the first stage of the project, but I am pleased that you have since opened it up to all age groups. I think it is important for the project to seek to reach a wider community.

In fact something I have often wondered is whether the project would benefit from including other professions beyond the creative industries. I love the energy that creatives bring, but I feel that other businesses could potentially provide more structure to trainees.

Tenant Jonathan Nyati in discussion with his trainee Pierre

CO: I agree—though the mix of tenants has really worked and the skills they bring to the project are incredible, I could imagine that businesses that work more on a nine-to-five model would work well in terms of offering trainees the stability that they need. It would also work well with social enterprises. Many of the businesses we have at the Studios are starting out and though they are all incredibly promising, they themselves are still struggling to find their own paths.

ML: Part of what excited me about the project was the idea of creating something based on an alternative economy, an economy that rejected the exchange of money and instead opted for another model. My only reservation with this is how sustainable it can be.

CO: Well we have just celebrated our one-year anniversary and have been awarded further funding for another year from Brent Council. Naturally the long-term fate of the project is still not secure and we still have some thinking to do about whether we introduce nominal rent in the future and how this will affect the way we run traineeships, but we are pretty positive that we could adapt the model to suit if need be.

ML: I think the important thing to also note is that this project wouldn't have been possible without the seed funding offered by the South Kilburn Neighbourhood Trust. In a time of government cuts across the board I hope the Studios can be seen as an example of how a little government investment can go a long way. I always enjoyed that element of the project – showcasing the way that creativity can give a lot back if given a little. I hope that is something that the Number 10 Downing Street advisors took away with them when they visited the project last year!

CO: Well, we can only hope, can't we? In the meantime we will carry on improving on the Studios model, carving out our place withing South Kilburn and maintaining a commitment to its regeneration.

ABOUT THE DELIVERY PARTNERS

SOUTH KILBURN NEIGHBOURHOOD TRUST

SKNT was founded in December 2008. The Trust is in an excellent position to take forward the legacy of the SKNDC/SKP programme in 2011. Ongoing work in 2010/11 has focused on developing a business plan, establishing funding arrangements and influencing the priorities in the South Kilburn 15 year Registration Strategy. The Trust has already taken a lead position in bringing about the capital regeneration of the South Kilburn area by acquiring opportunity sites for housing development (the old Texaco site on Carlton Vale) and will work with Catalyst to develop up to forty new homes for local people here.
www.skpartnership.net

THE ARCHITECTURE FOUNDATION

Founded in 1991 as the UK's first independent architecture centre, The Architecture Foundation is a non-profit agency for contemporary architecture, urbanism and culture. We cultivate new talent and new ideas. Through our diverse programmes we facilitate international and interdisciplinary exchange, stimulate critical engagement among professionals, policy makers and a broad public, and shape the quality of the built environment. We are independent, agile, inclusive and influential. Central to our activities is the belief that architecture enriches lives.
www.architecturefoundation.org.uk

PRACTICE ARCHITECTURE

Practice Architecture was founded in 2008 by Lettice Drake and Paloma Gormley who were joined by Henry Stringer in 2009. Fundamental to their approach to architecture is an involvement in every stage of a project – from inception through to construction and installation – with people. They make their buildings themselves, assisted by a small team of friends and volunteers who, like Practice Architecture, learn on the job. This construction principle shapes the design process, favouring low-tech materials and buildings with a strong internal logic, capable of being made by a relatively unskilled work force. Although driven by pragmatism, the integral relationship between how their architecture is made and by whom, amounts to a whole philosophy of design: buildings are made according to a human scale; there is continuity between the means of construction and its subsequent use; and specialisation is rejected for trans-disciplinary skills and an architecture that harnesses the energy and expression of a community.
www.practicearchitecture.co.uk

CORE TEAM, FOUNDING TENANTS AND TRAINEES

THE ARCHITECTURE FOUNDATION

Sarah Ichioka
Moira Lascelles

PRACTICE ARCHITECTURE

Lettice Drake
Paloma Gormley
Henry Stringer
Olga Winterbottom

SOUTH KILBURN NEIGHBOURHOOD TRUST

Sarah Butler
Peter Webster

BRENT COUNCIL

Alex Hearn
Abigail Stratford

GRAPHIC DESIGN

Joe Porter
Work + Play

PHOTOGRAPHY

Mike Massaro

FOUNDING TENANTS

Benjamin Stefanski
Bob Clarke
Caren Owen
Dan Rolfe Johnson
Jacob Tomkins
Daniel Thomas
Emily Evans
Josh Grigg
Jack Patterson
Jonathan Nyati
Mike Massaro
Kit Oates
Eleanor Kelly
Patrizia Victor
Victoria Grant
Tatiana von Preussen
Catherine Pease
Jessica Reynolds
Kieren Jones
Will Shannon

FOUNDING TRAINEES

Glenroy Ranger
Gary Brennan
Fancisco Rebello
Junior Maduako
George Allawi
Faith Galiwango
Jack Brindley
Sebastian Ferrao
Ferdos Mohammed
Ravi Chandarana
Pierre Blaire
Sarah Nansambadah
Julio Rebello
Tee Esen
Josh Wilton-Regan

ACKNOWLEDGEMENTS

Willmott Dixon Housing, Denne Construction, AKT II Engineers and Travis Perkins.

Alex Rennie, Abigail Stratford from Brent Council, Dan Thompson and Workshop 24, Deepak Chavda, Simon Rochowski, Dougald Hine of Space Makers, Concrete Canvas Arts, the Granville Arts Club, the OK Club, Terry Dackombe from Job Centre Plus, Jonathan Nyati, Aster Mehari, Spike Hudson, Vale Marini, Theo Mensah, Jessica Wear, Fran Box, Mike Massaro, Tommi Zhou, Paul Leathers, Paloma Strelitz, Josh Grigg, Jack Patterson, Will Shannon, Matthew Drage, Polly Gardiner, Sue Cooper, Sharif Said, Lena McManus, Steve Rowe, Dave Fish, Steven Matthews, Peter Clarke, Lorraine Lane, Jane Mumford, Matthew Turner, Catalyst Housing Group, Abdi Abdullah, Ammon Nwagbo, Annachiara Legnani, Annette Madsen, Anup Chavda, Ardit Berdica, Barney Lee, Barry Mcgurk, Caroline Koon, Cliff Mpuka, Curtis Clough, Dan Chandler, Dick Patterson, Gent Karaxha, Iqbal Uddin, Jason Malipol, Joshua Ponchiana, Khaled Korda, Lena Nemanus, Lucy Duncan, Lyndon Harrisson, Mary Mollison, Michale O'Donahue, Mohamed Dore, Paul Leathers, Roki Hussain, Tansy Drake, Besnik Ajvazi, Mohamed Dore, Gent Karaxha, Kalid Korda, Waleed Merza, Cliff Mpaka, Jean O'Mahoney, Katie Duncan, Olivia Chessell, John Bingham-Hall, Will Salmon, Mathew Cunningham, Lucy Duncan, Milly Suiter, Dan Rolfe Johnson and those whose names we did not manage to catch.

Sarah Trounce, David Crowe and Gerrie van Noord for their work on this publicaiton.

SK STUDIOS

www.southkilburnstudios.org